What Is The Duty Of Pious Men In Regard To Freemasonry?

Aug. C. L. Arnold

Kessinger Publishing's Rare Reprints

Thousands of Scarce and Hard-to-Find Books on These and other Subjects!

- Americana
- Ancient Mysteries
- Animals
- Anthropology
- Architecture
- Arts
- Astrology
- Bibliographies
- Biographies & Memoirs
- Body, Mind & Spirit
- Business & Investing
- Children & Young Adult
- Collectibles
- Comparative Religions
- Crafts & Hobbies
- Earth Sciences
- Education
- Ephemera
- Fiction
- Folklore
- Geography
- Health & Diet
- History
- Hobbies & Leisure
- Humor
- Illustrated Books
- Language & Culture
- Law
- Life Sciences
- Literature
- Medicine & Pharmacy
- Metaphysical
- Music
- Mystery & Crime
- Mythology
- Natural History
- Outdoor & Nature
- Philosophy
- Poetry
- Political Science
- Science
- Psychiatry & Psychology
- Reference
- Religion & Spiritualism
- Rhetoric
- Sacred Books
- Science Fiction
- Science & Technology
- Self-Help
- Social Sciences
- Symbolism
- Theatre & Drama
- Theology
- Travel & Explorations
- War & Military
- Women
- Yoga
- *Plus Much More!*

We kindly invite you to view our catalog list at:
http://www.kessinger.net

THIS ARTICLE WAS EXTRACTED FROM THE BOOK:

Rationale and Ethics of Freemasonry

BY THIS AUTHOR:

Aug. C. L. Arnold

ISBN 0766126900

READ MORE ABOUT THE BOOK AT OUR WEB SITE:

http://www.kessinger.net

OR ORDER THE COMPLETE
BOOK FROM YOUR FAVORITE STORE

ISBN 0766126900

Because this article has been extracted from a parent book, it may have non-pertinent text at the beginning or end of it.

CHAPTER XIV.

The Duty of Pious Men to Freemasonry.

THE Society of Freemasons is not a *club* of reckless, fun-loving men, who repudiate all that is serious, and ridicule all the grace of piety—it is a body of earnest men, intelligent men, good and true men, who love Virtue, reverence Religion, and worship God. And besides, the arrangements of the Order have been adapted with special reference to their religious and moral bearing. The great fact—the sentiment of accountability—which underlies all religions, which may claim to be divine, is the central idea, around which all our ceremonies revolve—the fountain whence all our moral lessons are drawn! There is not a rite in our Order which does not look backward to the Creator, and forward to eternity—which does not forth-shadow some of the profoundest mysteries of the Soul, and contribute directly to man's moral growth.

The moral and religious aspects of the institution should recommend it to the attention and love of all serious-minded men.

But another reason presents itself, still more

powerful, perhaps. Let it be observed that, in the United States alone, there must be an almost unnumbered multitude of them. Let it also be observed that these are all men for the most part in active life—a majority of them probably heads of families, and all of them together commanding an influence which reaches to, and affects directly, nearly one million of persons! And the circle of this influence is ever enlarging! It is not a superficial, transient influence, but deep and abiding—thousands and tens of thousands are governed by it, sustained by it, and consoled by it! Here, then, in the very heart of the community, is a mighty and ever-increasing power, which *must* and *will* control the destinies of millions! This power is an existing fact—this influence is now in active operation all around us—for good or for evil, it *will* make itself felt. Think of this, Christians, who love Virtue, Humanity, and God, and consider well whether you are not in duty bound to give your countenance to the Order—to direct it by your wisdom, and govern it by your virtue; and thus bind it indissolubly to the cause of good morals and religion.

The influence of Masonry is, must, and will continue to be widely felt; and if you have fears and doubts with respect to the character of that influence, come with us, labor with us, and secure to this body a healthy influence. For ourselves, we have

264   THE DUTY OF PIOUS MEN TO FREEMASONRY.

no fears, no doubts, as to the practical workings and ultimate results of Freemasonry. And were you, the good, the wise, the religious—all associated with us, the bare supposition of evil results would be impossible; while anticipations of great and incalculable good would be absolutely certain.

Printed in the United States
101863LV00003B